THE FIGURE IN THE MIRAGE

Robert Hichens

[ZHINGOORA BOOKS]

This edition is published by
Zhingoora Books.

On a windy night of Spring I sat by a great fire that had been built by Moors on a plain of Morocco under the shadow of a white city, and talked with a fellow-countryman, stranger to me till that day. We had met in the morning in a filthy alley of the town, and had forgathered. He was a wanderer for pleasure like myself, and, learning that he was staying in a dreary hostelry haunted by fever, I invited him to dine in my camp, and to pass the night in one of the small peaked tents that served me and my Moorish attendants as home. He consented gladly. Dinner was over—no bad one, for Moors can cook, can even make delicious caramel pudding in desert places— and Mohammed, my stalwart *valet de chambre*, had given us most excellent coffee. Now we smoked by the great fire, looked up at the marvellously bright stars, and told, as is the way of travellers, tales of our wanderings.

My companion, whom I took at first to be a rather ironic, sceptical, and by nature "unimaginative globe-trotter—he was a hard-looking, iron-grey man of middle-age—related the usual tiger story, the time-honoured elephant anecdote, and a couple of snake yarns of no special value, and I was beginning to fear that I should get little entertainment from so prosaic a sportsman, when I chanced to mention the desert.

"Ah!" said my guest, taking his pipe from his mouth, "the desert is the strangest thing in nature, as woman is the strangest thing in human nature. And when you get them together—desert and woman—by Jove!"

He paused, then he shot a keen glance at me.

"Ever been in the Sahara?" he said.

I replied in the affirmative, but added that I had as yet only seen the fringe of it.

"Biskra, I suppose," he rejoined, "and the nearest oasis, Sidi-Okba, and so on?"

I nodded. I saw I was in for another tale, and anticipated some history of shooting exploits under the salt mountain of El Outaya.

"Well," he continued, "I know the Sahara pretty fairly, and about the oddest thing I ever could believe in I heard of and believed in there."

"Something about gazelle?" I queried.

"Gazelle? No—a woman!" he replied..

As he spoke a Moor glided out of the windy darkness, and threw an armful of dry reeds on the fire. The flames flared up vehemently, and I saw that the face of my companion had changed. The hardness of it was smoothed away. Some memory, that held its romance, sat with him.

"A woman," he repeated, knocking the ashes out of his pipe almost sentimentally—"more than that, a French woman of Paris, with the nameless charm, the *chic*, the—— But I'll tell you. Some years ago three Parisians—a man, his wife, and her unmarried sister, a girl of eighteen, with an angel and a devil in her dark beauty—came to a great resolve. They decided that they were tired of the Français, sick of the Bois, bored to death with the boulevards, that they wanted to see for themselves the famous French colonies which were for ever being talked about in the Chamber. They determined to travel. No sooner was the determination come to than they were off. Hôtel des Colonies, Marseilles; steamboat, *Le Général Chanzy*; five o'clock on a splendid, sunny afternoon—Algiers, with its terraces, its white villas, its palms, trees, and its Spahis!"

"But——" I began.

He foresaw my objection.

"There were Spahis, and that's a point of my story. Some fête was on in the town while our Parisians were there. All the African troops were out—Zouaves, chasseurs, tirailleurs. The Governor went in procession to perform some ceremony, and in front of his carriage rode sixteen Spahis—probably got in from that desert camp of theirs near El Outaya. All this was long before the Tsar visited Paris, and our Parisians had never before seen the dashing Spahis, had only heard of them, of their magnificent horses, their turbans and flowing Arab robes, their gorgeous figures, lustrous eyes, and diabolic horsemanship. You know how they ride? No cavalry to touch them—not even the Cossacks! Well, our French friends were struck. The unmarried sister, more especially, was *bouleversée* by these glorious demons. As they caracoled beneath the balcony on which she was leaning she clapped her little hands, in their white kid gloves, and threw down a shower of roses. The falling

flowers frightened the horses. They pranced, bucked, reared. One Spahi—a great fellow, eyes like a desert eagle, grand aquiline profile—on whom three roses had dropped, looked up, saw mademoiselle—call her Valérie—gazing down with her great, bright eyes—they were deuced fine eyes, by Jove!—
—"

"You've seen her?" I asked.

"—and flashed a smile at her with his white teeth. It was his last day in the service. He was in grand spirits. 'Mem Dieu! Mais quelles dents!' she sang out. Her people laughed at her. The Spahi looked at her again— not smiling. She shrank back on the balcony. Then his place was taken by the Governor— small imperial, *chapeau de forme*, evening dress, landau and pair. Mademoiselle was *désolée*. Why couldn't civilised men look like Spahis? Why were all Parisians commonplace? Why—why? Her sister and brother-in-law called her the savage worshipper, and took her down to the café on the terrace to dine. And all through dinner mademoiselle talked of the *beaux* Spahis—in the plural, with a secret reservation in her heart. After Algiers our Parisians went by way of Constantine to Biskra. Now they saw desert for the first time—the curious iron-grey, velvety-brown, and rose-pink mountains; the nomadic Arabs camping in their earth-coloured tents patched with rags; the camels against the skyline; the everlasting sands, broken here and there by the deep green shadows of distant oases, where the close-growing palms, seen from far off, give to the desert almost the effect that clouds give to Cornish waters. At Biskra mademoiselle—oh! what she must have looked like under the mimosa-trees before the Hôtel de l'Oasis!———"

"Then you've seen her," I began.

"—mademoiselle became enthusiastic again, and, almost before they knew it, her sister and brother-in-law were committed to a desert expedition, were fitted out with a dragoman, tents, mules—the whole show, in fact—and one blazing hot day found themselves out in that sunshine—you know it—with Biskra a green shadow on that sea, the mountains behind the sulphur springs turning from bronze to black-brown in the distance, and the table flatness of the desert stretching ahead of them to the limits of the world and the judgment day."

My companion paused, took a flaming reed from the fire, put it to his pipe bowl, pulled hard at his pipe—all the time staring straight before him, as if, among the glowing logs, he saw the caravan of the Parisians winding onward across the desert sands. Then he turned to me, sighed, and said:

"You've seen mirage?"

"Yes," I answered.

"Have you noticed that in mirage the things one fancies one sees generally appear in large numbers—buildings crowded as in towns, trees growing together as in woods, men shoulder to shoulder in large companies?"

My experience of mirage in the desert was so, and I acknowledged it.

"Have you ever seen in a mirage a solitary figure?" he continued.

I thought for a moment. Then I replied in the negative.

"No more have I," he said. "And I believe it's a very rare occurrence. Now mark the mirage that showed itself to mademoiselle on the first day of the desert journey of the Parisians. She saw it on the northern verge of the oasis of Sidi-Okba, late in the afternoon. As they journeyed Tahar, their dragoman—he had applied for the post, and got it by the desire of mademoiselle, who admired his lithe bearing and gorgeous aplomb—Tahar suddenly pulled up his mule, pointed with his brown hand to the horizon, and said in French:

"'There is mirage! Look! There is the mirage of the great desert!'

"Our Parisians, filled with excitement, gazed above the pointed ears of their beasts, over the shimmering waste. There, beyond the palms of the oasis, wrapped in a mysterious haze, lay the mirage. They looked at it in silence. Then Mademoiselle cried, in her little bird's clear voice:

"'Mirage! But surely he's real?'

"'What does mademoiselle see?' asked Tahar quickly.

"'Why, a sort of faint landscape, through which a man—an Arab, I suppose—is riding, towards Sidi—what is it?—Sidi-Okba! He's got something in front of him, hanging across his saddle.'

"Her relations looked at her in amazement.

"'I only see houses standing on the edge of water,' said her sister.

"'And I!' cried the husband.

"'Houses and water,' assented Tahar. 'It is always so in the mirage of Sidi-Okba.'

"'I see no houses, no water,' cried mademoiselle, straining her eyes. 'The Arab rides fast, like the wind. He is in a hurry. One would think he was being pursued. Why, now he's gone!'

"She turned to her companions. They saw still the fairy houses of the mirage standing in the haze on the edge of the fairy water.

"'But,' mademoiselle said impatiently, 'there's nothing at all now—only sand.'

"'Mademoiselle dreams,' said Tahar. 'The mirage is always there.'

"They rode forward. That night they camped near Sidi-Okba. At dinner, while the stars came out, they talked of the mirage, and mademoiselle still insisted that it was a mirage of a horseman bearing something before him on his saddle-bow, and riding as if for life. And Tahar said again:

"'Mademoiselle dreams!'

"As he spoke he looked at her with a mysterious intentness, which she noticed. That night, in her little camp-bed, round which the desert winds blew mildly, she did indeed dream. And her dream was of the magic forms that ride on magic horses through mirage.

"The next day, at dawn, the caravan of the Parisians went on its way, winding farther into the desert. In leaving Sidi-Okba they left behind them the last traces of civilisation—the

French man and woman who keep the auberge in the orange garden there. To-day, as they journeyed, a sense of deep mystery flowed upon the heart of mademoiselle. She felt that she was a little cockle-shell of a boat which, accustomed hitherto only to the Seine, now set sail upon a mighty ocean. The fear of the Sahara came upon her."

My companion paused. His face was grave, almost stern.

"And her relations?" I asked. "Did they feel——"

"Haven't an idea what they felt," he answered curtly.

"But how do you know that mademoiselle

"You'll understand at the end of the story. As they journeyed in the sun across the endless flats—for the mountains had vanished now, and nothing broke the level of the sand—mademoiselle's gaiety went from her. Silent was the lively, chattering tongue that knew the jargon of cities, the gossip of the Plage. She was oppressed. Tahar rode close at her side. He seemed to have taken her under his special protection. Far before them rode the attendants, chanting deep love songs in the sun. The sound of those songs seemed like the sound of the great desert singing of its wild and savage love to the heart of mademoiselle. At first her brother-in-law and sister bantered her on her silence, but Tahar stopped them, with a curious authority.

"'The desert speaks to mademoiselle,' he said in her hearing. 'Let her listen.'

"He watched her continually with his huge eyes, and she did not mind his glance, though she began to feel irritated and restless under the observation of her relations.

"Towards noon Tahar again described mirage. As he pointed it out he stared fixedly at mademoiselle.

"The two other Parisians exclaimed that they saw forest trees, a running stream, a veritable oasis, where they longed to rest and eat their *déjeuner*.

"'And mademoiselle?' said Tahar. 'What does she see?'

"She was gazing into the distance. Her face was very pale, and for a moment she did not answer. Then she said:

"'I see again the Arab bearing the burden before him on the saddle. He is much clearer than yesterday. I can almost see his face——'

"She paused. She was trembling.

"'But I cannot see what he carries. It seems to float on the wind, like a robe, or a woman's dress. Ah! *mon Dieu!* how fast he rides!'

"She stared before her as if fascinated, and following with her eyes some rapidly-moving object. Suddenly she shut her eyes.

"'He's gone!' she said.

"'And now—mademoiselle sees?' said Tahar.

"She opened her eyes.

"'Nothing.'

"'Yet the mirage is still there,' he said.

"'Valérie,' cried her sister, 'are you mad that you see what no one else can see, and cannot see what all else see?"

"'Am I mad, Tahar?' she said gravely, almost timidly, to the dragoman.

"And the fear of the Sahara came again upon her.

"'Mademoiselle sees what she must,' he answered. 'The desert speaks to the heart of mademoiselle.'

"That night there was moon. Mademoiselle could not sleep. She lay in her narrow bed and thought of the figure in the mirage, while the moonbeams stole in between the tent pegs to keep her company. She thought of second sight, of phantoms, and of wraiths. Was this riding Arab, whom she alone could see, a phantom of the Sahara, mysteriously accompanying the caravan, and revealing himself to her through the medium of the mirage as if in a magic mirror? She turned restlessly upon her pillow, saw the naughty moonbeams, got up, and went softly to the tent door. All the desert was bathed in light. She gazed out as a mariner gazes out over the sea. She heard jackals yelping in the distance, peevish in their insomnia, and fancied their voices were the voices of desert demons. As she stood there she thought of the figure in the mirage, and wondered if mirage ever rises at night—if, by chance, she might see it now. And, while she stood wondering, far away across the sand there floated up a silvery haze, like a veil of spangled tissue—exquisite for a ball robe, she said long after!—and in this haze she saw again the phantom Arab galloping upon his horse. But now he was clear in the moon. Furiously he rode, like a thing demented in a dream, and as he rode he looked back over his shoulder, as if he feared pursuit. Mademoiselle could see his fierce eyes, like the eyes of a desert eagle that stares unwinking at the glaring African sun. He urged on his fleet horse. She could hear now the ceaseless thud of its hoofs upon the hard sand as it drew nearer and nearer. She could see the white foam upon its steaming flanks, and now at last she knew that the burden which the Arab bore across his saddle and supported with his arms was a woman. Her robe flew out upon the wind; her dark, loose hair streamed over the breast of the horseman; her face was hidden against his heart; but mademoiselle saw his face, uttered a cry, and shrank back against the canvas of the tent.

"For it was the face of the Spahi who had ridden in the procession of the Governor—of the Spahi to whom she had thrown the roses from the balcony of Algiers.

"As she cried out the mirage faded, the Arab vanished, the thud of the horse's hoofs died in her ears, and Tahar, the dragoman, glided round the tent, and stood before her. His eyes gleamed in the moonlight like ebon jewels.

"'Hush!' he whispered, 'mademoiselle sees the mirage?'

"Mademoiselle could not speak. She stared into the eyes of Tahar, and hers were dilated with wonder.

"He drew nearer to her.

"'Mademoiselle has seen again the horseman and his burden.'

"She bowed her head. All things seemed dream-like to her. Tahar's voice was low and monotonous, and sounded far away.

"'It is fate,' he said. He paused, gazing upon her.

"'In the tents they all sleep,' he murmured. 'Even the watchman sleeps, for I have given him a powder of hashish, and hashish gives long dreams—long dreams.'

"From beneath his robe he drew a small box, opened it, and showed to mademoiselle a dark brown powder, which he shook into a tiny cup of water.

"'Mademoiselle shall drink, as the watchman has drunk,' he said—'shall drink and dream.'

"He held the cup to her lips, and she, fascinated by his eyes, as by the eyes of a mesmerist, could not disobey him. She swallowed the hashish, swayed, and fell forward into his arms.

"A moment later, across the spaces of the desert, whitened by the moon, rode the figure mademoiselle had seen in the mirage. Upon his saddle he bore a dreaming woman. And in the ears of the woman through all the night beat the thunderous music of a horse's hoofs spurning the desert sand. Mademoiselle had taken her place in the vision which she no longer saw."

My companion paused. His pipe had gone out. He did not relight it, but sat looking at me in silence.

"The Spahi?" I asked.

"Had claimed the giver of the roses."

"And Tahar?"

"The shots he fired after the Spahi missed fire. Yet Tahar was a notable shot."

"A strange tale," I said. "How did you come to hear it?"

"A year ago I penetrated very far into the Sahara on a sporting expedition. One day I came upon an encampment of nomads. The story was told me by one of them as we sat in the low doorway of an earth-coloured tent and watched the sun go down."

"Told you by an Arab?"

He shook his head.

"By whom, then?"

"By a woman with a clear little bird's voice, with an angel and a devil in her dark beauty, a woman with the gesture of Paris—the grace, the *diablerie* of Paris."

Light broke on me.

"By mademoiselle!" I exclaimed.

"Pardon," he answered; "by madame."

"She was married?"

"To the figure in the mirage; and she was content."

"Content!" I cried.

"Content with her two little dark children dancing before her in the twilight, content when the figure of the mirage galloped at evening across the plain, shouting an Eastern love song, with a gazelle—instead of a woman—slung across his saddle-bow. Did I not say that, as the desert is the strangest thing in nature, so a woman is the strangest thing in human nature? Which heart is most mysterious?"

"Its heart?" I said.

"Or the heart of mademoiselle?"

"I give the palm to the latter."

"And I," he answered, taking off his wide-brimmed hat—"I gave it when I saluted her as madame before the tent door, out there in the great desert."

End of the book.